Let Me
TALK MY ISH

Let Me TALK MY ISH

GIGI WHITAKER

Book Cover Design:

Sophisticated Press LLC

ISBN 978-1-7371743-0-1

PRINTED IN THE UNITED STATES OF AMERICA

Published by GIGI WHITAKER

Publishing Consultant

SP

SOPHISTICATED
P R E S S

In Dedication to My Hero,

Jesse L. Coleman.

Acknowledgments

Wow, where do I begin?! Of course, without a doubt THE CREATOR! Everything I am is because of You. You see fit to continuously bless me in spite of myself. Thank you for this vision and for allowing me to achieve one of my long-term goals, becoming an author. Continue to use me. To my one and only, my ace, my rider, my sidekick, my mini-me, my reason, my Legacy.... Mommy could never express in words the love I have for you, and what you mean to me. You are my reason for it all. You are not only my greatest accomplishment, but my greatest blessing. I'm not sure what I did for God to see fit to make me your mother, but I am so grateful to have you ride shotgun on this journey called life. Keep applying pressure, baby girl. To my publishing company, Sophisticated Press, and my mentor throughout this journey, Renetta. You are truly heaven-sent. There is no way my vision would have come to life without your patience, and guidance. So many times I wanted to pull the plug on this project, and then I'd talk to you and quickly realize quitting was not an option. Thank you for your energy and all that you do. To my parents, thank you for your unconditional love and nurturing me from a girl, to a young lady, to a woman. Your sacrifices over the years have never gone unnoticed, and I promise it's coming back tenfold. Nanny, I wish you were here to see what your "Flea" has been up to. But I know you've been right by my side not missing a beat. I just hope I'm making you proud. My granny, I love you, I love you, I love you. I've never seen a woman so strong. You are the glue to the "Coleman Clan". We would be lost without you. To my siblings, thanks for putting up with me all these years. Lol I know it was hard having a little sister so dope. Lol, I love you all more than you all could ever know. My nieces and nephew TiTi will forever have your backs. I love yall like a fat kid loves cake. To my tribe, you know who you are. The stories we could tell. Smh Lol We've laughed, cried, fussed, and even cursed, but most importantly we've loved. The loyalty and support you all show goes unmatched. When I say I got you I got you! It's only up from here... There are so many people I would like to thank and acknowledge that had no clue they were even a part of this project. I kept this project a secret during its development just because I wanted to surprise everyone with its release. My goal is as always, to make you all proud, and I hope I have done that.

Love,
-GiGi

Table of Contents

BOSS TALK

1

BOSS TALK

Life is a b*#ch, so I made her a business woman...

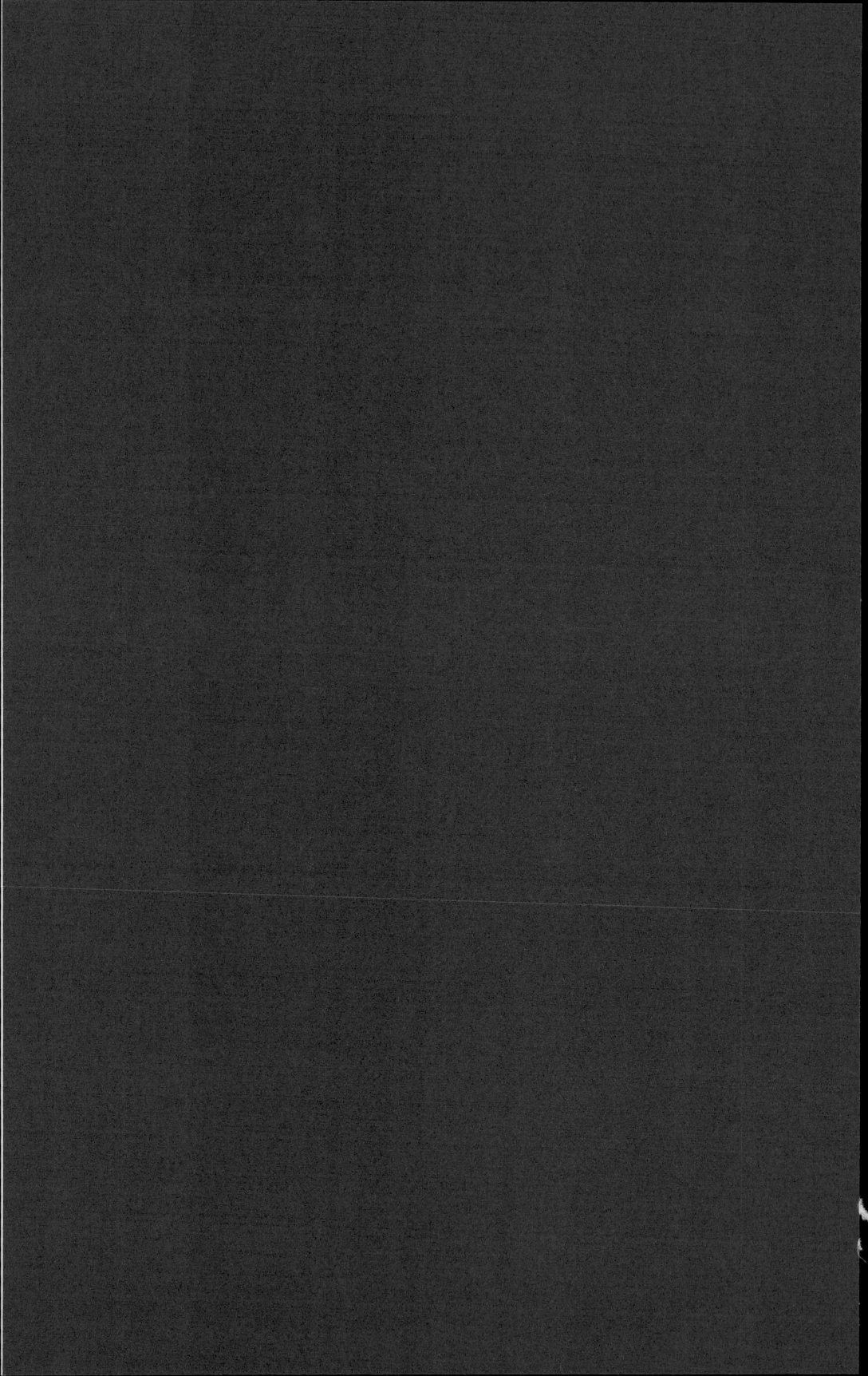

- Bitter is a broke chick trait. I can't relate. 💅
- It's winter year-round dealing with me. 🥶 I've never met one that's colder.
- I'm not bossy, I am THE boss! 💪
- You can't play me without playing yourself. So, make your next move your best move 🙂
- Getting cash is my #1 task. 💵 Mission complete!
- I would call myself Barbie, but I'm nothing to be played with. 💋
- It costs to be the boss, and you coming up short.
- Believe the hype!
- Bosses don't roll in packs.
- This what they been waiting for, so I'm gone serve 'em from head to toe. 💃 🤩
- What ceiling? 👻 I'm breaking every boundary.
- There's what you're used to, and then there's me. 💅
- Keep the safe secure like I do these bundles. 🏦 😀
- No one going hard as me, 💪 resume on steroids. 💊
- I follow checks, not trends. 💵
- When I say I'm out of pocket I'm not talking about my finances. 🙂
- This that pressure have a lame brain dead. 💭
- I'm tired of being modest, refer to me as goddess. 🧕
- Maybe I'm really too much to handle, breaking these dudes down like enamel. 🦷 😁

- Got 'em all watching me like, "That's what I want to be!" 😃
- You asked to see the boss, so they sent me. 💪
- Shit could get ugly. That's why God made me pretty. 🏽
- You can keep the clout, I prefer the coins. 🪙
- I can't see nobody but me. Who I'm gone lose to? 🥴
- I never call myself the GOAT. I leave that up to the people.
- Trying to stay grounded, but I keep taking flight. 🛫
- I ain't never been used, unless it was for motivation.
- Life is a b*#ch, so I made her a businesswoman. 👰 💼
- I was making 'em sick before COVID.
- I'm the rookie, and the vet. 🏆 Show some respect!
- Bump their opinion, they ain't see the vision.
- I took the lead now they all follow. 🏃 🚶 🚶
- This shit ain't for everybody!
- She keep'em sweating like they in a hotbox. 😰
- I'm a vibe you want to catch!
- Don't try this at home! This drip is for experts.
- I think of myself so highly, cause I don't just get paid Friday.
- Y'all can keep the tea. I prefer the juice! 🧃
- They upset cause they ain't seen me fall yet.
- They tried to downplay my dreams. So, I give it to 'em every time I step on the scene.
- Hustle like I got something to prove.
- I got that green in my eyes like I'm Donnie Simpson. 💵

- While my name in your mouth don't forget to add, but she gets to the bag! 💰
- If it ain't about the money I ignore it. 😎
- Simon says I'm still that chick!
- Call me Crisco cause I pop my ish! 💥
- I been fine it just gets better with time. ⏰
- It's me..... I'm the caption! 👄
- I been getting fine, while the pockets getting fluffy. 💰
- You couldn't see me if you had floor seats. 💺
- Throwing money like its shade. 💸
- When you a boss you don't be getting in gossip, you just get in your bag. 💰
- Your rent money my play money, 💰 and it's about time for recess.
- The ticket going up, 🔼 can't be accessible to everybody.
- I'm up counting money while y'all counting sheep. 🐑
- We don't speak the same language. My shit is expensive! 💴 💶 💷
- When you at the top of course they gone look up to you.
- Tell your people make a shirt for you cause I'm killing you chicks. ☠️
- I'm so high maintenance that you lames can't contain me.
- The rules to checkers don't apply in the game of chess. ♟️
- Yall get high off the life I live. 😵
- Like a genie, I got em all wishing. 🧞

- If I were you I'd hate me too.
- You could study my every move and still not know me. 😊
- Money like a drug to me, I think I'm about to relapse.
- I'm my own goals! 🤩
- The all-stars start and end the game. 😌
- No need to get on a scale, they already know I'm heavy. 💪
- I ain't telling time with another's watch. I'm in a league of my own.
- Walk in the meeting and they see money. 🤑 I'm a walking investment.
- The money is straight, so I don't have to worry about it coming out the closet.
- You can see it on my face, I'm a Boss 25/8.
- Lil baby tried to keep up, messed around and went broke.
- I'm goal getter!
- Since they can't sit with me they don't want to see me eat, but little did they know my plate already made. 🍽
- I take selfies cause I don't see nobody but me.
- She don't catch feelings she too busy catching flights. 🛫
- Big boss chick! 💪 I don't come in your size.
- Call me Meek cause I'm on my way to a mill. 💰
- Call me novocaine cause I'm numb to the bull.
- I keep my own self draped in Gucci and gold.
- I'm not the type you get over.
- Don't need a pen or paper I'm gone still draw attention. 💋

- Can't complain my table full when my goal was to eat.
- So outta this world they think I play for the Astros. 🚀
- I don't dance, but I definitely make moves.
- I was grinding all them nights while y'all were in bed, Imma get it all until the day I'm dead. 😵
- Money, Power, Respect.....3 The Hard Way!
- I keep shit low. Everybody on a need to know.
- You choose your fate with me. Just make sure you can pay the price.
- Ten toes down while you falling off your feet.
- You know how I'm living I don't have to post it.
- I got em asking what does she do?" I do everything, and then some too.
- I make money, no need for friends.
- They be wishing on a star I would quit, but they just mad I ain't on the bench.
- Look like heaven, but I be giving em hell 😈.
- I don't have a bad side, so I'm not pressed for angles.
- I get dressed in Louis just to go shopping at Gucci.
- I don't ride the wave, I create it 🌊.
- Card got so many charges it's been indited 💳.
- I talk big ish like the CAPS Lock on ⬆️.
- Better check my temperature I was hot before the summer 😷.
- Why chase you when I'm the catch 🐆

- If getting money is a sin then Im destined for hell. 🔥
- Didn't your teacher tell you to keep your eyes on your own paper. 💵
- A woman with drive can never be put in park. 💋
- They'll remember my name because I created my own lane. 🪦
- I could be your lesson or your blessing. Choose wisely!
- If he a baller I'm gone put him on the team.
- On my Mekhi Phifer ish. Pay me in full!
- I don't do this for fun, I do it for funds. 💵
- Got more drive than Uber and Lyft together. 🚗 🚗
- More sauce than your favorite pasta dish. 🍯
- I'm a problem that nobody's solving.
- If your mind always on me how you thinking bout your money? 🗿 💰 Reroute your energy, love!
- Married to the money, so it's easy to be monogamous 💍 💵
- Scared money don't make money, and yall are looking frightening. 😱
- I could give you the playbook, and you still couldn't stop me.
- Maybe I'm high maintenance, or maybe you're just low effort.
- I'm Lawrys with the black pepper, fully seasoned with no effort.

- If you ever see me run from the heat cut my legs off. The kitchen ain't never been too hot for me.
- Treating my past like a ponytail .... leaving it behind me.
- No silver spoons were used in the process. This that muddy water drip.
- I'm not bougie, I was just raised correctly.
- I'm not bougie. I'm blessed.
- You can tell by my look I ain't lacking. 🥾🔒🔪
- You can follow behind but u can't cheat the grind.
- Hard to sleep on me like a twin bed. 💤🛏️
- Don't mind me. I'm just reading scriptures, and getting richer. 📖💰
- Face so pretty they think I got work. 💉
- They think I endorse Burger King because I be having things my way.
- Throwing salt on my name will only season my sauce. 🧂🍯
- Keep throwing stones, and watch the empire I build with them. 🧱
- Everybody screaming boss, but ain't got a staff. Bosses put others in a better position.
- Gotta show the positives for those that can't add.
- They trying to figure out how to drive in my lane, while I'm closing deals on a plane. 🛩️💸💳
- I'm always in the running cause the marathon continues. 🏁

- All that hating and you still lost, now you mad cause I'm still a boss. 💪
- Call me Mrs. Claus cause I got the gift. 🎅
- I'm the table and the chairs. Don't get it twisted!
- Your first mistake was counting me out.
- I ain't gotta be woke to be up. 🥱
- It's not fair to put a lion against a lamb. So quit comparing yourself.
- I can provide the plate, but I can't eat for you. 🍽️
- Look at me, this is how you wear a mortgage. 🤑
- Don't study me because you won't graduate. 📚
- Good things take time, that's why I'm always late.
- Even with instructions you wouldn't know what to do with me. 📖
- We don't pay the same taxes. 'Nough said!
- I was a boss before I could post about it. ✍️
- I ain't working out but I'm pushing up. 🏆
- Tested positive for being the illest!
- I'm gone keep going up the ladder and make em madder. 💪
- I put on my jewelry when I want to cool down. 💎
- I'm not from Georgia but I'm holding a peach. 🍑 😛
- Them: She's trash. Me: Better believe this bag is heavy. 💪
- They thought I fell off. Whole time I was loading up. 😖 💪
- I don't dream, I make it a reality. 💬

- On or offline I'm dope. 🖊️😷
- I got the cake like it's my birthday. 🎂
- I don't compete because I've already won.
- I would say I'm Gucci, but I prefer Louis. 😆 👜
- I might spend all four seasons at the Four Seasons. I ain't trying to flex I do it without a reason. 💪🍁🍀🌼❄️
- Time is money, check the bezel. ⏱️
- Feeling myself can't murder my ego.
- You don't worry about being the black sheep when youre the GOAT.
- I couldn't be touched before there was COVID.
- Keeping it cute has never been a problem for me, 🖊️ I do that effortlessly.
- Making moves without needing a uhaul.
- Hustle bananas 🐒, you can't peel this back.
- Stunting on my enemies 🤸 cause they said I'd never make it.
- If you take off now you still couldn't catch up. 🏃
- They only throw salt when you pose a threat
- I don't do beef, I prefer cabbage. 💰
- If it ain't about a blessing I can't address it.

TRUST LOYALTY SLAY

BESTIE
TALK

2

BESTIE TALK

He wants to take me on trips, but
only if he fly out the crew...

- It's a homies only kind of mood.
- The party doesn't start until we show up. 🎉
- Aint no switching sides. 🔁
- Known to keep the baddest on my team.
- One thing all my girls have in common are dead presidents. 🤑
- He wants to take me on trips, but only if he fly out the crew .✈️
- Still running with the same ones til the death of me. 🕯️
- My team play in a whole nother league.
- Bump good, we demand great!
- My real ones gone show me love, while the hating ones wish for a hug. 🫂
- I don't deal with losers or lames. I can't afford any Ls. 👻
- We ain't for the streets. We just be outside sometimes. 🏏♂️

3

SHADY TALK

You can be anything in the world,
but yet you chose me...

- If I ever wanted your man he was took. Got so much tea ☕ I could write a book 📖
- Saw your new girl and it boost my self-esteem. 😂
- The chosen one while you try your best to be seen. ✏️
- She's a keeper, too bad you didn't keep her. 💋
- Audacity must be on sale this season, everybody seems to have it.
- You can be anything in the world, but yet you chose me. 😵
- You chicks don't apply enough pressure to intimidate me. 😝
- I act like I don't notice, but I keep it noted. 📝
- You'll probably find someone, but you'll never find a me. 😵
- You ain't really living that shit you said 😵. It be the capping for me.
- Only time I play around is when I'm with your man. 💀
- Be yourself! I'm already taken.
- Stay in your lane, or you may get ran over. 🚗
- Got me thinking the envy was in your heart from the start, had to cut you off cause you couldn't play your part.
- I'm not arrogant, I'm just out of your reach! 😎
- They rather hate vs being a fan!
- Your insufficient vibes let me know you can't pay attention. 😄
- This ain't sesame street, I can't kick it with you birds. 🦅

- Sometimes the ones you want to stunt with are the ones you have to stunt on. 🐵
- You can't compete where you don't compare! ✏️
- Keep taking notes sis! 📝 But it ain't enough ink to copy this drip.
- They trying to compete when they can't even compare.
- They talking, but ain't saying nothing. 😶
- I'm the whole loaf, you the breadcrumbs. 🍞
- Keep my feet greased so they're shining on their necks. 💥
- They don't like you, but won't dare unfollow you. 🙁
- Don't take a loss you can't afford trying to keep up with me, this is a different league right here.
- Gone drop a😴 while you're lurking. Yall give me ops vibes.
- They want to be just like me. Poor thing that's highly unlikely.
- On these chicks minds like a bonnet.
- You ain't a baddie. You just doing bad!
- I do what I want, while you do what you can.
- The only thing a chick can take from me is notes. 📝
- The hate always comes from the bleachers never the court. The players are too busy playing the game while the spectators try their best to distract them.
- Running circles around the one you think is the best, 🏆 and I ain't even done yet.

- The wack ones always try to act like they don't know who I am, but my name stay in their search bar.
- They be dissing, but wishing they could come for my position. 💪
- Maybe if you try a little harder you wouldn't have to try so hard.
- Beware of the ones that act friendly in person, then be online trying to sneak diss. 🙄
- If I got you mad now, you gone cry later. 😠 😥
- You looking real jealous... You probably don't mean it, but just can't help it.
- It hurts some of you to see me, but yet you still won't close your eyes. 👀
- I'm gone have my way, and yours too! 😬
- I ain't Nick Cannon, but I will wild out!
- I see you looking. Now watch what I do. 👀
- Can't be around a salty bih. I have high blood pressure. 😄
- You dumb if you lose me, I'm my own investment.
- They know I'm the shit that's why they hate me like Chris.
- They don't like me but stay in my views. 🙄
- You lames couldn't beat me with lotion.
- Everybody say they solid, but so is ice until you apply heat. 🧊
- No need for revenge when your absence gone kill em.
- Pissing em off so much I suggest they stay hydrated. 💦

- I'm gone start selling water since they stay thirsty. 🐙
- Being salty causes hypertension... Don't be a salty bih!
- They scream ride or die, but won't even start the car. 😒
- If you see me running know I'm on my victory lap! 🏳
- I'm the ex he don't regret! 😛
- Popping lames like tags! 🗨 💥
- On you bums nerves like a toothache. 🦷 😫
- They talking shit with less than 4 accomplishments. I got too much to lose.
- I can bag ya man just by posting a pic. 📷
- They bopping! I do it they copy. 😀
- Aight let me get my foot off y'all neck. 🦶 I see the pressure too much.
- They want to ride my wave, but do better calling an uber. 🌊 🚗
- In these chicks head like a sew-in.
- They'll love you, but hate on your hustle.
- I'm cautious cause some of my old ones crossed me. ⚠
- You bums easy like Sunday morning.
- Don't be on social media acting like you want smoke knowing you have asthma. 😮
- Don't let your fingers type some ish you can't get out of. 📟
- I'm a blessing to you lames like I sneezed on you. 👻
- I'm spiritual, but I will set it off like I'm Vivica Fox!
- They look at me as a problem, too bad they can't solve it.

- Mad cause I found out the real you, cut you off cause I ain't feel you. ✂️
- Be his peace... he already wishes you were me! ☮️
- Y'all gotta stop quoting Moneybagg Yo when you're the penny. 🔔
- Trying to do what I do..You can't fake this!
- Y'all give me mannequin vibes.... fake dummies!
- You get hype about a blue check. Meanwhile, I'm writing/cashing checks. We are not the same! ✅
- If I hit his line he gone curve her like a pitch. ⚾
- They block me but still jock me!
- You're a trip, I'm a vacation... our destinations aren't the same.
- I don't have enemies, just cheerleaders that ain't cheering.
- I speak the truth but that's a foreign language to the masses.
- Them: she makes me sick Me: let me get you a room with the other patients.
- Argue with your edges, not me!
- You acting out but ain't nobody here for the show.
- I'm not vegan, so I want all the beef!
- They don't like me, but know everything that I do. 🙄
- Your MCM jewelry can't get wet but you call me fake. 🙄 😵
- Stop trying to figure out how I do what I do, when I ain't even worried about you. 🙄

- They hate to see me prosper, so they won't even bless me when I sneeze.
- They line up for me like they copping the Js!
- You wouldn't catch my shade if you weren't in my shadow.
- I'm trying to live my life like it's golden, and y'all giving me bronze vibes. 😵
- You're #2 in your own lane, and I ain't even competing.
- Everybody has a job, I guess their position is to hate. 🙊
- You chasing a dude, I'm chasing a tax bracket. We are not the same! 💰
- I got em feeling some type of way, so they get on Twitter and type away. ⌨️
- I seen you fall for a goofy, that's when I knew I wasn't your type.
- Judging by your finances, I can see green isn't your color.
- I don't expect you to like me, you don't even like yourself.
- May God have mercy on those that crossed me because I won't.
- The unbothered ones have the most to say. 🙄
- Any beef with me I suggest you chew and swallow. 🍖
- Call me the goat cause I give you all hope.
- They try to compete, but can't even play on the same court. 🏀
- I got the miles, but I'm not tripping.

- Call me Toni Braxton cause I make it where you can't breathe again.
- You can ask your baby father, I'm flyer than his baby mother.
- It's cheaper to keep her, but not me though.

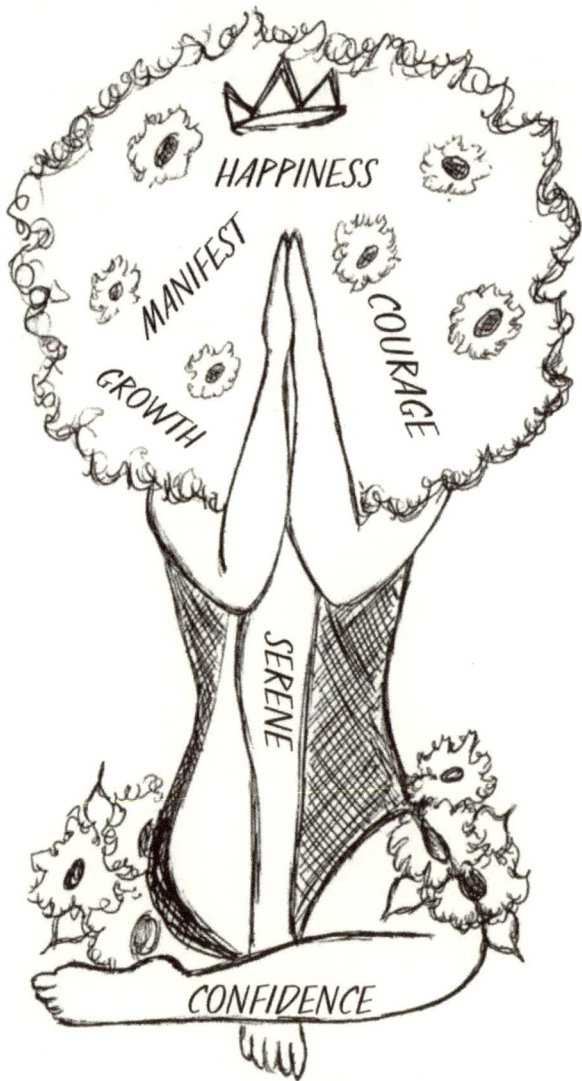

4

MOTIVATION TALK

No one can unseat you at a table
God has prepared in your favor.

- The pressure will either make you a diamond, or make you fold.... The choice is yours!
- I am a money manifester! ✳️
- Don't put dead situations on life support. Pull the plug!
- Make that pain art!
- You have to take some losses to win. 🏆
- You only lose when you don't swing back.
- Believe in yourself more than your angles.
- Head high cause I'm holding up my crown. 👑
- The more consistent you are, the more consistent your money. 💰
- Expect a check, not debt! 💵
- Just because they don't want you at the table doesn't mean you don't deserve a seat. 🪑
- Chase your dream, and the bag will come.
- You have to level up if you want it. 💪
- Good things don't always come the way you expect them.
- Put the power in your own hands.
- Pain is just an investment for progress.
- No one can unseat you at a table God has prepared in your favor.
- We only regret the change we didn't make.
- Your confidence is the best fashion statement.
- The ones that doubt you will be the same ones that need you.

- Their opinions are not your reality.
- If you don't aim too high, then you're aiming too low.
- I might bend a little bit, but I don't break.
- Never take what they give you. Take what you're owed.
- Stop taking advice from someone who can't even look at their reflection.
- You can't dull a sparkle. ✳️
- I'm a combo deal. The outside is beauty. The inside is peace.
- Some will look at you with hate in their eyes. Others with respect... but either way they're looking. 👀
- Don't adapt to the energy in the room. Be the energy in the room.... you're a whole vibe, sis 🖤.

COUPLES TALK

5

COUPLES TALK

We don't need vacations cause I'm his favorite getaway...

- Treat her like you're still trying to win her, and you'll never lose her. 👩‍🦰👨‍🦰
- I prayed for you 🙏 you're the example that dreams do come true.
- If it makes you happy it doesn't have to make sense to others.
- We ain't picture perfect but we're worth a picture still. 📷
- How'd he do it I don't know, but somehow I got hooked. 🪝
- I don't really gamble, but for you I'll roll the dice. 😊🎲
- This may be the winning hand of all the times I played 👊dealt them cards to me now we off to foreign lands.
- Call me an addict because I'm addicted to this loving.🤞
- Wrapped around you like a turban. 👺
- It's rare you find someone who sees the same world you see. 👊 🔒
- If his name on it, mine right beside it. 👊👯Teamwork makes the dream work.
- If you don't see a leader in him, then you're being misled.
- They can't shake us, nor break us. 👊🔒
- I ain't perfect it's true, but I'm perfect for you.
- Had them other chicks mad when they seen us. Matching whips baby, team us.
- I been getting to the new money with my old one. 😊
- If it's his, it's mine!

- They be dissing and wishing they could come for my position. 😕 ✏️
- When he a boss he don't be getting in gossip, he just gone get to the money.💵
- Whatever I want I know he gone cop it. 😣
- When I say I got you that's off my intuition. So he say he got me, and my tuition. 📖 💰 💪
- Even if we're on the run we gone chase our dreams as one.
- His co-defendant if necessary, so don't let the necessary occur 😐.
- The one he don't regret! 😋
- Every locked thing has it's key 🔐 and for him it's me!
- I can be a saint and a sinner, but yet you still singing me praises.
- I won't play with your mind, but I just might blow it. 😶
- It ain't fun if it's easy.
- You can look, but don't touch. 💂
- I'm all of his vices in one. 😊
- Like words to a melody, we just flow together. 🎶
- He don't deal with dimes, only 20s! 🔲
- Look like heaven, but I be giving him hell. 😇 😈
- We don't need vacations cause I'm his favorite getaway.🏝️
- What's better for you than me?! 😕
-
- Always by his side like a glock .45.

36

- I'm his new obsession.
- Let's put the bs behind us and go somewhere they can't find us. 🏞️🏕️⛰️
- I'm his blessing like I sneezed on him. 👻
- We ain't no angels, but heaven is on our side.
- You gotta be a queen when you're riding with a king. 👑
- He said I'm like a perc cause I get him high.
- It's Me for him!
- Some things are just better together. 👌

About The Author

GiGi Whitaker resides in Houston, TX where she was born, and raised. She is the mother of one to an exceptionally talented daughter. Before writing, GiGi received her bachelor's degree in psychology from the University of Houston. Her love for fashion led her to start her consignment/personal shopping service, The Treasure Trunk Houston. In her spare time, GiGi can be found traveling the world, cooking, or reading.

If you would like to know when GIGI WHITAKER books are released, please visit www.letmetalkmyish.com, where you can sign up for updates and new releases.

www.ingramcontent.com/pod-product-compliance
Lightning Source LLC
Chambersburg PA
CBHW031226090426
42740CB00007B/733

9 781737 174301